D1489124

365
Mindful
Days…

A daily thought on being
present in the now

edited by Dalton Exley
illustrations by Angela Kerr

MJF BOOKS | New York

Published by MJF Books
Fine Communications
589 Eighth Avenue, 6th Floor
New York, NY 10018

365 Mindful Days
LC Control Number: 2018953802
ISBN 978-1-60671-430-0

Printed in China.

MJF Books and the MJF colophon are trademarks
of Fine Creative Media, Inc.

[1010]   10   9   8   7   6   5   4   3   2   1

MINDFULNESS CAN be summed up in two words: *pay attention.* Once you notice what you're doing, you have the power to change it.

MICHELLE BURFORD

THE SOUL always knows what to do to heal itself.
The challenge is to silence the mind.

CAROLINE MYSS, B. 1952

To BE content with what we possess is the
greatest and most secure of riches.

MARCUS TULLIUS CICERO
106–43 B.C.

WE ARE the Earth, through the plants and
    animals that nourish us.
We are the rains and the oceans that flow
    through our veins.
We are the breath of the forests of the land,
    and the plants of the sea.
    . . .
Linked in that web, we are interconnected . . .

D. T. SUZUKI
1870–1966

MINDFULNESS IS like waking from a long
hibernation and suddenly seeing a world
so beautiful it takes your breath away.

DR. DALTON EXLEY

THIS IS it. No one else has the answer. No
other place will be better, and it has already
turned out. At the center of your being you
have the answer; you know who you are
and you know what you want.

LAO TZU
C. 604–531 B.C.

THE SECRET of the future is here in the present. . . .
Each day, in itself, brings with it an eternity.

PAULO COELHO, B. 1947

Do EVERY act of your life as
if it were your last.

MARCUS AURELIUS
121–180

STOP SEARCHING. Find. Stop asking. Just do.
Stop worrying. Relax. Stop being anxious—about
the past, about the future. Just be you. Just do
what you do. Live your life. Just be.

DR. DALTON EXLEY

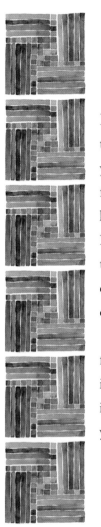

The Mindfulness Exercise

BE AWARE of your breath, of breathing: there's nothing "to do." Be mindful of your breathing, that's all. Sit with both feet on the ground, your hands on your lap. Bring all your attention to breathing. Notice the air entering your nose, going to your lungs and leaving again. This exercise isn't about relaxation, but this is often a welcome side effect.

Become an observer of yourself. Do this for a few minutes each day, don't time it, just do this till you've had enough of it—even noting thoughts as they pop into your head.

THE WORLD is round and the place which
may seem like the end may also
be the beginning.

IVY BAKER PRIEST
1905–1975

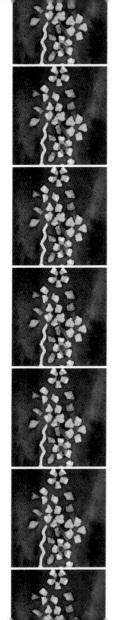

As YOU simplify your life, the laws
of the universe will be simpler;
solitude will not be solitude,
poverty will not be poverty, nor
weakness weakness.

HENRY DAVID THOREAU
1817–1862

HE WHO always speculates as to what awaits him in future, accomplishes nothing whatsoever.

SWAMI VIVEKANANDA
1863–1902

To BE at peace, make peace with your life,
with everything. Know peace in every day, in
every moment. You'll find it is like when a tap
is dripping you notice it more when it stops.
And you will find a burden lifted from
you, with a lightness of being that is as
effortless as a smile . . .

Dr. Dalton Exley

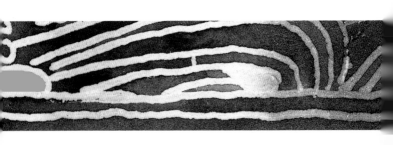

JOY IS a single moment, an eternal
Now, in which wonder and beauty
are unfathomable, inexhaustible,
a peace and an astonishment.

PAM BROWN
1928–2014

A SHAFT of sunlight at the end of a dark afternoon,
a note in music, and the way the back of a baby's neck
smells . . . Those are the important things.

E. B. WHITE
1899–1985

EACH MOMENT is absolute, alive, and significant. The frog leaps, the cricket sings, a dewdrop glitters on the lotus leaf, a breeze passes through the pine branches and the moonlight falls on the murmuring stream.

D. T. SUZUKI
1870–1966

IF EVERY eight-year-old in the world is taught meditation, we will eliminate violence from the world within one generation.

THE DALAI LAMA,
B. 1935

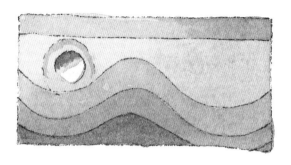

NOTHING EVER gets anywhere. The earth keeps turning round and gets nowhere. The moment is the only thing that counts.

JEAN COCTEAU
1889–1963

MINDFULNESS IS the aware, balanced acceptance of the present experience. It isn't more complicated than that. It is opening to or receiving the present moment, pleasant or unpleasant, just as it is, without either clinging to it or rejecting it.

SYLVIA BOORSTEIN, B. 1936

IF WE are not in this present millisecond of life
and conscious experience, we are not alive; we
are merely thinking our lives. Yet we have seen so
many die, looking back over their shoulders at
their lives, shaking their heads and muttering in
bewilderment, "What was that all about?"

STEPHEN LEVINE
1937–2016

About Mindfulness Exercises

If you do mindfulness exercises and start applying them to daily life the results can be astounding. Many people say they cope better, overcoming deep tensions and negative tendencies. Rather than going through life on autopilot, influenced by past experiences, they find themselves clearer minded and calmly assertive, developing a fully conscious mind, freer from self-limiting repetitive thought processes. Mindfulness helps us become fully present in the now, focusing on positive directions for our lives.

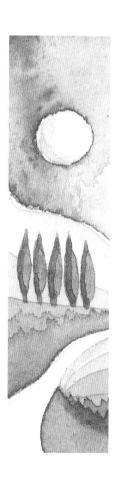

TODAY IS all we
ever really have.
Make the most of
it, treasure it.

DR. DALTON EXLEY

ALWAYS HOLD fast to the present. Every situation, indeed every moment, is of infinite value, for it is the representative of a whole eternity.

JOHANN WOLFGANG VON GOETHE
1749–1832

MINDFULNESS SIMPLY means being aware,
being present. When you are breathing
and know that you are breathing, that is
mindfulness of breathing.

SOREN GORDHAMER

ONE OF the conclusions I have come to in my old age is the importance of living in the ever-present now. In the past, too often I indulged in the belief that somehow or other tomorrow would be brighter or happier or richer.

RUTH CASEY

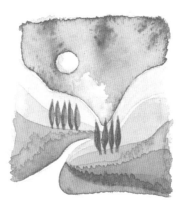

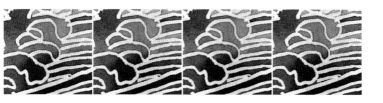

THE SECRET of health for both mind and body is not to mourn for the past, not to worry about the future, or not to anticipate troubles, but to live the present moment wisely and earnestly.

GAUTAMA BUDDHA

C. 563–483 B.C.

PEACE OF mind produces right values, right values
produce right thoughts. Right thoughts produce
right actions and right actions produce work which
will be a material reflection for others to see of the
serenity at the center of it all.

ROBERT M. PIRSIG
1928–2017

TEN THOUSAND flowers
in spring, the moon in
autumn, a cool breeze
in summer, snow in winter.
If your mind isn't clouded
by unnecessary things,
this is the best season
of your life.

WU-MEN
1183–1260

Find times to let your guard down,
to fully surrender to the moments
as they pass you by. Your life will be
richer for it.

Dr. Dalton Exley

EVERY DAY is a birthday; every moment
of it is new to us; we are born again,
renewed for fresh work and endeavor.

ISAAC WATTS
1674–1748

TRY TO be mindful, and let things take their natural course. Then your mind will become still in any surroundings, like a clear forest pool. All kinds of wonderful, rare animals will come to drink at the pool, and you will clearly see the nature of all things.

ACHAAN CHAH
1918–1992

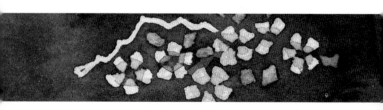

THERE IS great happiness
in not wanting, in not being
something, in not going
somewhere.

JIDDU KRISHNAMURTI
1895–1986

Each second you can be reborn.
Each second there can be a new
beginning. It is choice, it is
your choice.

Clearwater

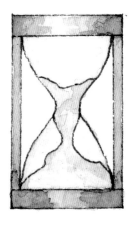

You do not need to leave your room.
Remain sitting at your table and listen. Do not even
listen, simply wait. Do not even wait, be quiet, still
and solitary. The world will freely offer itself
to you to be unmasked. It has no choice.
It will roll in ecstasy at your feet.

Franz Kafka
1883–1924

RELAX. ENJOY the
journey. We're not
coming back again.

DR. DALTON EXLEY

THE SOIL was soothing, strengthening,
cleansing and healing. That is why the old
Indian still sits upon the earth instead of
propping himself up away from its life-
giving forces. For him, to sit or lie upon the
ground is to be able to think more deeply
and feel more keenly.

LUTHER STANDING BEAR, OGLALA SIOUX CHIEF
1868–1939

WE COLLECT data, things, people, ideas, "profound experiences," never penetrating any of them . . . But there are other times. There are times when we stop. We sit still. We lose ourselves in a pile of leaves or its memory. We listen and breezes from a whole other world begin to whisper.

JAMES CARROLL, B. 1943

IF ALL the clocks were
stopped, what time would
it be?

ZEN WISDOM

A Mindfulness Eating Exercise

CHOOSE SOME food you like, maybe a piece of fruit or chocolate. Imagine you've never seen it before, explore it 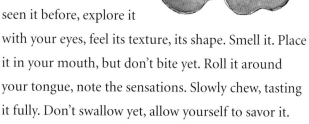 with your eyes, feel its texture, its shape. Smell it. Place it in your mouth, but don't bite yet. Roll it around your tongue, note the sensations. Slowly chew, tasting it fully. Don't swallow yet, allow yourself to savor it. Finally, be aware of the feeling of swallowing. This is mindful eating.

LIFE ISN'T just about counting the days until you can retire, nor is it about counting your money, it's about making every moment count.

SUZE ORMAN, B. 1951

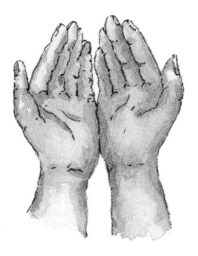

THERE ARE two days every week you
don't have to worry about. Yesterday and
tomorrow. And if you live today, that's
three. And if you keep doing this, that's
seven good days of every week.
That can't be bad.

DR. DALTON EXLEY

FOR ME the greatest beauty always lies in the
greatest clarity.

GOTTHOLD EPHRAIM LESSING
1729–1781

THE TRUTH is the most obvious thing, yet we are always looking for a needle in a haystack. When you see the Truth, nothing changes. A tree is still a tree, a mountain is a mountain.

KARLFRIED GRAF DÜRCKHEIM
1896–1988

"RENEW THYSELF
completely each day; do
it again, and again, and
forever again."

ON THE BATHTUB OF
KING TCHING THANG
1748–1799

LET GO.
Empty yourself.
Become quiet,
clear and calm.

YING-AN, D. 1163

WE'RE SO busy watching out
for what's just ahead of us that
we don't take time to enjoy
where we are.

BILL WATTERSON, B. 1958

MINDFULNESS HELPS us focus on one
thing at a time. Be it this moment in time,
or one goal you have. It helps you be
patient, find peace, focus, find kindness,
find creative awareness, whatever you
choose, it is your mindfulness.

DR. DALTON EXLEY

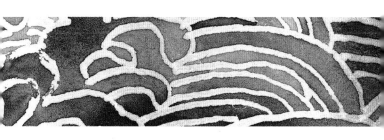

FLOW WITH whatever may happen and
let your mind be free. Stay centered by
acceptance. This is the ultimate.

LAO TZU

C. 604–531 B.C.

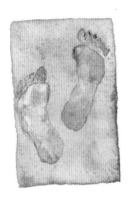

EVERY STEP that is taken
upon the earth should be
as a prayer.

BLACK ELK, OGLALA SIOUX
1863–1950

THE BEST and sweetest
things in life are things
you cannot buy: the music
of the birds at dawn, the
rainbow in the sky. The
dazzling magic of the stars,
the miracle of light.

PATIENCE STRONG
1907–1990

An Awareness of Nature Exercise

THIS SIMPLE exercise helps us to connect with the beauty of the natural world that we so often miss as we rush about our busy days. Choose something natural; it could be a flower, a tree, an insect or clouds in the sky. Focus on this and relax. Look at it as if for the first time, explore every aspect of it. Breathe. Allow yourself to connect with the natural world.

IF YOU really take to being mindful, then don't stop with yourself. Treat everyone you meet as mindfully as you do yourself. That moves the practice of a possibly slightly narcissistic obsession (certainly somewhat self-centered) to something truly remarkable. Treat a pauper, a king, a lover, a stranger with the same mindfulness as you treat yourself.

DR. DALTON EXLEY

WE ARE always getting ready to live,
but never living.

RALPH WALDO EMERSON
1803–1882

EACH MOMENT is magical, precious
and complete, and will never exist
again. We forget that now is the
moment we are in, that the next
one isn't guaranteed.

SUSAN L. TAYLOR, B. 1946

THE THING which we speak of as beauty
does not have to be sought in distant
lands... It is here about us or it is
nowhere...

ALLEN TUCKER
1866–1939

A daily thought on being present in the now

THE GREATEST revelation is stillness.

LAO TZU

C. 604–531 B.C.

To MY mind anyone who turns away from nature, whose head is forever filled with thoughts of keeping up this and keeping up that . . . oh, going on like that, one so easily arrives at a point where one can no longer tell white from black.

VINCENT VAN GOGH
1853–1890

To THE mind that is still, the
whole universe surrenders.

LAO TZU
C. 604–531 B.C.

LIVING MINDLESSLY takes an
enormous toll.

ROGER WALSH, B. 1946

I'M FILLED with joy when the day dawns quietly over
the roof of the sky.

ESKIMO LOVE SONG

A daily thought on being present in the now

LISTEN IN deep silence. Be very still, and open your mind. . . . Sink deep into the peace that waits for you beyond the frantic, riotous thoughts and sounds and sights of this insane world.

FROM *A COURSE IN MIRACLES*

NONE OF us can ever go back in time
and start anything again. What we can
all do, if we want to, is start again from
now and make a brand-new ending.

DR. DALTON EXLEY

A WISE person does not value a large jade but cherishes a moment of time, for time is difficult to keep and very easy to lose.

CHINESE SAYING

SIT
Rest
Work.

Alone with yourself,
Never weary.

On the edge of the forest
Live joyfully,
Without desire.

GAUTAMA BUDDHA
C. 563–483 B.C.

MAY THIS be one of the days
. . . when the mind discovers
undreamed-of things. . . . when the
eye is overwhelmed by glory. . . .
may this be one of the days
of new beginning when we seem
to see to the very edges of the
universe.

PAM BROWN
1928–2014

Happy the man, and happy he alone,

He who can call today his own:

He who, secure within, can say,

Tomorrow do thy worst, for I have lived today.

John Dryden
1631–1700

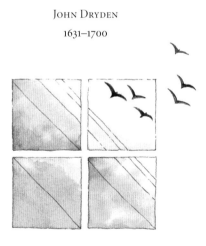

DON'T BE so good at preparing for the future, at planning, planning, planning, that you forget to live today. In all this planning—planning for promotion, or to get a better car, or a bigger house, or greater wealth—everything is for tomorrow.
All those todays sacrificed for tomorrows.

DR. DALTON EXLEY

ALL MY possessions for one moment of time.

QUEEN ELIZABETH I
1533–1603

THE BIRDS have vanished down the sky.
Now the last cloud drains away.

We sit together, the mountain and me,
until only the mountain remains.

LI PO
701–762

I EXPAND and live in the warm day like
corn and melons.

RALPH WALDO EMERSON
1803–1882

I BELIEVE that life should be lived so vividly
and so intensely that thoughts of another life, or
of a longer life, are not necessary.

MARJORY STONEMAN DOUGLAS
1890–1998

ALL THAT we are is the result of what we
have thought. The mind is everything.
What we think we become.

GAUTAMA BUDDHA C. 563–483 B.C.

I HAVE no magic power; I make inward strength my
   magic.

. . .

I have no friends; I make my mind my friend.

I have no enemy; I make incautiousness my enemy.

I have no armor; I make goodwill and righteousness
   my armor.

I have no castle; I make immovable Mind my castle.

THE SAMURAI'S CREED

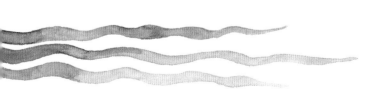

THOSE IN a hurry do not arrive.

ZEN WISDOM

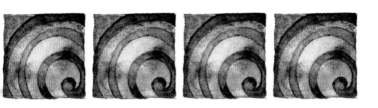

JUST STILL the thoughts in your
mind. It is good to do this right in the
midst of disturbance.

YUAN-WU
1063–1135

THAT IT will never come again
Is what makes life so sweet.

EMILY DICKINSON
1830–1886

LIVE THE present. Do the things you
know need to be done. Do all the
good you can each day. The future
will unfold.

PEACE PILGRIM
1908–1981

MINDFULNESS IS being in the now without wishing it were different. It is enjoying the good things of life as well as feeling the unpleasant—but it is not over-dwelling on these things. Through this process the everyday can come to seem miraculous and our problems are placed more in perspective. It is an awakening.

DR. DALTON EXLEY

A Mindfulness of Physical Discomfort Exercise

FOCUS YOUR attention on breathing. Just observe. Then shift attention to your body—which areas are comfortable, which uncomfortable? See if you can feel those different sensations. If thoughts pop into your head, observe, but don't act on them. Notice how sensations shift, or diminish your attention to other areas of discomfort. To close, bring your attention back to your breathing. Many people are astonished that by simply being aware of discomforts, they lessen. Try it.

BREATHE OUT, look in, let go.

JOHN WELWOOD, B. 1943

Though we travel the world over to find the beautiful, we must carry it with us or we find it not.

Ralph Waldo Emerson
1803–1882

EVERY DAY, stop before something beautiful long
enough to say, "Isn't that beautiful!"

ALICE FREEMAN PALMER
1855–1902

TRY DYING every day to
your old self . . . so that you
emerge renewed and young
again as the tired mind
sheds its load . . .

KRISTIN ZAMBUCKA,
B. 1941

A Mindful,
Stillness Exercise

FIND A quiet place you can sit comfortably. Place
your hands palm up and open on your knees. Either
close your eyes, or leave them open. Begin by paying
attention to your breath. Inhale. Exhale. Just be
aware of your breath . . . Think of becoming calm,
quiet, letting go of any tensions and thoughts. Allow
calmness, tranquility and peace to surround you. Stay
still and be aware of your breath . . .

DEEP IN the soul, below pain, below
all the distraction of life, is a silence vast
and grand—an infinite ocean of calm,
which nothing can disturb; Nature's
own exceeding peace, which "passes
understanding."

That which we seek with passionate
longing, here and there, upward and
outward, we find at last *within ourselves.*

C. M. C.

THE REAL meditation is how you live your life.

JON KABAT-ZINN, B. 1944

SOLITUDE, QUALITY
solitude, is an assertion of
self-worth, because only in the
stillness can we hear the truth
of our own unique voices.

PEARL CLEAGE, B. 1948

TODAY.

(ON A STONE ON JOHN RUSKIN'S DESK)
JOHN RUSKIN
1819–1900

RING THE bells that still can ring

Forget your perfect offering

There is a crack in everything

That's how the light gets in.

LEONARD COHEN 1934–2016

GRANTED, AN hour of sensory tuning-in at the beach,
by the stream, under the shade tree, on the nature trail,
or atop the windswept butte won't fix all the broken
stuff in our lives, but it will pull us out of our writhing
minds, and into our grounded, flowing senses.

PHILIP S. CHARD

MINDFULNESS SHOULDN'T be overcomplicated.
It is quite simple really—just be in the moment.
Oh, and remember to do it; that's all.

DR. DALTON EXLEY

I HAVE found such joy in things that fill
My quiet days: a curtain's blowing grace,
A potted plant upon my window sill,
A rose, fresh-cut and placed within a vase . . .

GRACE NOLL CROWELL
1877–1969

MINDFULNESS IS simply being aware of what is happening right now without wishing it were different; enjoying the pleasant without holding on when it changes (which it will); being with the unpleasant without fearing it will always be this way (which it won't).

JAMES BARAZ

NEVER BE in a hurry; do everything
quietly and in a calm spirit. Do not
lose your inner peace for anything
whatsoever, even if your whole world
seems upset.

SAINT FRANCIS DE SALES
1567–1622

JUST HAVE no mind on things and no
things in your mind, and you will naturally
be empty, spiritual, and sublime.

TE-SHAN
782–865

I WILL breathe.
I will think of solutions.
I will not let my worry
control me. I will not let
my stress break me. I will
simply breathe. And it
will be okay . . .

SHAYNE MCCLENDON

Don't overcomplicate mindfulness and make work out of it. We don't need to practice to enjoy the sunrise over mountains, or the sunset on a beach. What do we need to learn about the beauty of flowers and the deep blue of the sky?

Dr. Dalton Exley

GRANT YOURSELF a moment of peace and you will understand how foolishly you have scurried about. Learn to be silent and you will notice that you have talked too much. Be kind and you will realize that your judgment of others was too severe.

TSCHEN TSCHI JU

YOU SEE, we believe that through the quieting of the mind we are able to separate what is real and what isn't, what is ego and what is truth. It is like making butter; you keep churning and churning until the cream begins to separate. You must really work at churning a chaotic mind, learn to separate your thoughts from your true nature, and become a witness rather than a party to your destructive emotions. What you are left with is a natural state of joy.

KUTENLA, BUDDHIST MONK

EARTH TEACH me stillness as the grasses are
   stilled with light.
Earth teach me humility as blossoms are humble
   with beginning.
Earth teach me courage as the tree which stands
   all alone.
Earth teach me limitation as the ant which
   crawls on the ground.
Earth teach me freedom as the eagle which soars
   in the sky.
Earth teach me resignation as the leaves which
   die in the autumn.
Earth teach me regeneration as the seed which
   rises in the spring.
Earth teach me to forget myself as melted snow
   forgets its life.

UTE PRAYER

Being Nonjudgmental about Feelings

FEELINGS ARE often labeled good or positive (confident, brave, upbeat) or negative (fearful, angry, sad, depressive). In mindfulness feelings are not judged as good or bad, they just are what they are. We tend to find some emotions difficult, or uncomfortable, and others easier. Rather than feeling that we mustn't feel sad, or scared, or down, in mindfulness we simply observe these feelings and emotions with curiosity, nonjudgmentally accepting them.

Exercise:
Being Mindful of Your Thoughts

START WITH being mindful of your breath. Be quiet and still. Notice any thoughts that pop up. Don't judge or internalize these thoughts as good or bad, positive or negative. If you notice you are struggling with thinking about your thoughts, notice this too as just another thought. While you do this, imagine your thoughts floating by like clouds, or as words written on water. Go with this if it works for you. Watch as thoughts come and go, replaced by others. Bring yourself back to your breath to close this exercise.

It's the scent of the roses that fills the air,
    And the whispering wind blowing through my hair.
It's the sparkling dew drops on the ground,
    And the gurgling stream that makes hardly a sound.
It's the feel of the snowflakes that melt on my tongue.
    And the night owl calling to her young.

Elizabeth Anne de Grey

SEARCH YOUR heart and see the
way to do is to be.

LAO TZU
C. 604–531 B.C.

A daily thought on being present in the now

THOSE WHO are awake
live in a state of constant
amazement.

GAUTAMA BUDDHA
C. 563–483 B.C.

DRINKING TEA, eating rice,
Passing time as it comes;
Looking down at the stream,
Looking up at the mountain . . .

PAO-TZU

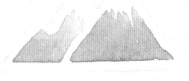

IF WE had keen vision of all that is ordinary in human life, it would be like hearing the grass grow or the squirrel's heart beat, and we should die of that roar which is the other side of silence.

GEORGE ELIOT (MARY ANN EVANS)
1819–1880

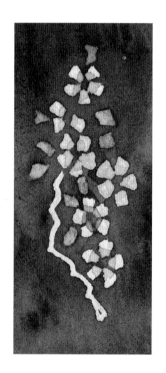

To FILL the hour—
that is happiness; to fill
the hour, and leave no
crevice for a repentance
or an approval.

RALPH WALDO EMERSON
1803–1882

PRAISE AND blame, gain and loss, pleasure and sorrow come and go like the wind. To be happy, rest like a great tree in the midst of them all.

GAUTAMA BUDDHA
C. 563–483 B.C.

WANTING IS the urge for the next moment to contain what this moment does not. When there's wanting in the mind, the moment feels incomplete. Wanting is seeking elsewhere. Completeness is being right there.

STEPHEN LEVINE
1937–2016

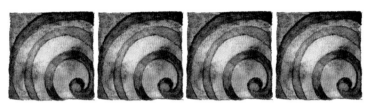

OH, THIS is the joy of the rose:

that it blows, and goes.

WILLA CATHER

1873–1947

BETWEEN THE stirrup and the ground there is always hope. Between stimulus and response there is always space. Therein lies our potential, our freedom, our choice, our growth.

DR. DALTON EXLEY

MY LIFE has no purpose, no direction, no aim,
no meaning and yet I'm happy. I can't figure it out.
What am I doing right?

CHARLES M. SCHULZ

1922–2000

Do NOT rage against the
world of the senses. Only by
accepting the world of the
senses can you share in
the true perception.

SENG-TS'AN
529–606

EVERY MINUTE life begins all over again.

THOMAS MERTON

1915–1968

BEGIN DOING what you want to do now. We are not living in eternity. We have only this moment, sparkling like a star in our hand—and melting like a snowflake.

SIR FRANCIS BACON
1561–1626

HERE ARE the veins of your hand and here are the veins of a leaf. Here branches stretch out against the sky. Here streams run to meet the river. We are bound together. The same life flows through all things. Be happy in this unity, this continuity.

PAM BROWN
1928–2014

HAPPINESS HAPPENS only in the present moment.
If you are happy now, there is nothing else to
accomplish. Indeed, if you become concerned about
whether you will be happy tomorrow or even five
minutes from now, you will forget to be happy now.
All your scheming and dreaming takes you away from
your present happiness.

PAUL FERRINI

I LAY in a meadow until the
unwrinkled serenity entered into
my bones, and made me into one
with the browsing kine, the still
greenery, the drifting clouds, and
the swooping birds.

ALICE JAMES
1848–1892

DON'T HURRY, don't worry. You're only here for a short visit. So be sure to stop and smell the flowers.

WALTER HAGEN
1892–1969

A daily thought on being present in the now

. . . HAPPINESS IS not simply a destination,
it is a method of traveling the road of life.

ELLEN R. WEINER

I WAS set free! I dissolved in the sea, became white sails and flying spray, became beauty and rhythm, became moonlight and the ship and the high dim-starred sky! I belonged, without past or future, within peace and unity and a wild joy, within something greater than my own life, or the life of Man, to Life itself!

EUGENE O'NEILL
1888–1953

OVER ALL the mountaintops is peace. In all treetops you perceive scarcely a breath. The little birds in the forest are silent. Wait then; soon you, too, will have peace.

JOHANN WOLFGANG VON GOETHE
1749–1832

How CAN I grasp it? No, do not grasp
it. Whatever remains when there is no
more grasping, is the self.

VIDYARANYA, *PANCHADASI*

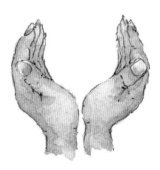

EVEN IN these rushed days there is such peace
between. There are moments when two eagle feathers
can fill me with joy; when the last rays of the sun touch
my forehead as I stand by the kitchen door . . . when
even the wind is part of it all. Surely such moments
do something to me. If not, it is because I hide
beneath the pettiness.

EDITH WARNER
1893–1951

TO RISE above treeline is to go above thought, and
after, the descent back into birdsong, bog orchids,
willows, and firs is to sink into the preliterate
parts of ourselves. It is to forget discontent,
undisciplined needs. Here, the world is only space,
raw loneliness, green valleys hung vertically.
Losing myself to it—if I can—I do not fall . . .

GRETEL EHRLICH, B. 1946

IT IS good to be alone in a garden at dawn or dark, so
that all its shy presences may haunt you and possess
you in a reverie of suspended thought.

JAMES DOUGLAS
1753–1819

THERE'S JOY all around us!
Why wait till tomorrow?
We've only this moment to live.
A heaven within us
Is ours for the finding,
A freedom no riches can give!

J. DONALD WALTERS
1926–2013

He is happiest, be he king
or peasant, who finds peace
in his home.

Johann Wolfgang von Goethe
1749–1832

I USED to believe that anything was better than nothing. Now I know that sometimes nothing is better.

GLENDA JACKSON, B. 1936

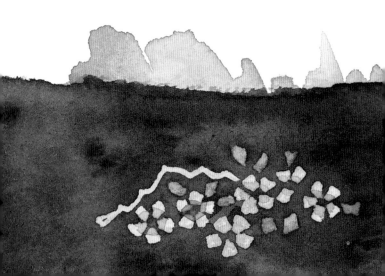

BEING IS born of not being.

LAO TZU

C. 604–531 B.C.

SITTING QUIETLY, doing nothing,
Spring comes and the grass grows by itself.

BASHO
1644–1694

. . . I KNOW of nothing else
   but miracles
. . .

To me, every hour of the light
   and dark is a miracle,

Every cubic inch of space is
   a miracle,

Every square yard of the surface
   of the earth is spread with
   the same,

Every foot of the interior
   swarms with the same . . .

WALT WHITMAN
1819–1892

THE USEFULNESS of a pot
comes from its emptiness.

LAO TZU

C. 604–531 B.C.

A Progressive Body Awareness Exercise

HERE'S AN exercise to become more aware of your body. Loosen tight clothing and lie in a comfortable position. Starting with your feet, notice any coolness, warmth, tightness, tension, comfort or discomfort. Simply notice and accept your body, whether in comfort or discomfort. Change your awareness to your legs, again noting any tightness or discomfort. Continue with your hips, stomach, chest, and back, hands, arms, shoulders, neck, head, mouth and tongue.

THE LURE of the distant and the difficult is deceptive.
The great opportunity is where you are.

JOHN BURROUGHS
1837–1921

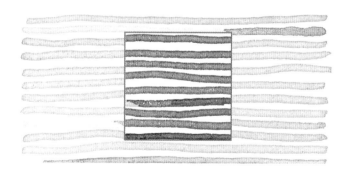

Einstein was right. You can live your life
as though nothing is a miracle or as though
everything is a miracle. You can see magic in the
tiniest atom right out to the entire unfathomable
universe, or you can just see the particular small
world of your existence. It is largely up to you
how you perceive the world.

Dr. Dalton Exley

IF THE doors of perception were cleansed everything
would appear to us as it is, infinite.

WILLIAM BLAKE
1757–1827

THE AIM of life is to live, and to live means to be aware, joyously, drunkenly, serenely, divinely aware.

HENRY MILLER
1891–1980

SOMETIMES, WHEN a bird cries out,
Or the wind sweeps through a tree,
Or a dog howls in a far-off farm,
I hold still and listen a long time.

My soul turns and goes back to the place
Where, a thousand forgotten years ago,
The bird and the blowing wind
Were like me, and were my brothers.

HERMANN HESSE
1877–1962

MAY YOU live each second with joy. May you live each minute with hope. May you live each hour with patience.

STUART & LINDA MACFARLANE

In Asian languages, the word for
"mind" and the word for "heart" are
the same. So if you're not hearing
mindfulness in some deep way
as heartfulness, you're not really
understanding it.

Jon Kabat-Zinn, b. 1944

GRADUALLY, A few moments one day, more moments
the next, being there in that small safe woodland began
to seem almost the same experience as making music,
as the way, when I played the piano, I was the music . . .
I had no consciousness of my individual self.

SALLY CARRIGHAR
1898–1985

IF YOU wish to advance into the infinite,
explore the finite in all directions.

JOHANN WOLFGANG VON GOETHE
1749–1832

NATURE IS painting
for us, day after day,
pictures of infinite beauty,
if only we have the eyes
to see them.

JOHN RUSKIN
1819–1900

WILLINGLY GREETING our fears and weaknesses with openness, acceptance, and respect is one of the hardest tasks mindfulness asks of us and one of the most freeing practices we can undertake. Sitting in stillness with our sorrow and shame, our fear and judgment laid bare is an act of courage.

SUE PATTON THOELE, B. 1940

THINK OF all this fleeting world:

A star at dawn, a bubble in a stream;

A flash of lightning in a summer cloud,

A flickering lamp, a phantom and a dream.

GAUTAMA BUDDHA
C. 563–483 B.C.

WHEN YOU realize that
you don't lack anything, that you
don't need anything, that
you can stop striving for what
you don't have all the time and
end this constant cycle of striving
and stress—it is like the world is
opened up before your eyes like
never before.

DR. DALTON EXLEY

To UNDERSTAND the
immeasurable, the mind must be
extraordinarily quiet, still.

JIDDU KRISHNAMURTI
1895–1986

SLOW DOWN and enjoy life. It's not only the scenery you miss by going too fast—you also miss the sense of where you're going and why.

EDDIE CANTOR
1892–1964

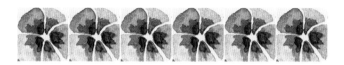

Don't evaluate your life in terms of achievements, trivial or monumental, along the way. . . . Instead, wake up and appreciate everything you encounter along the path. Enjoy the flowers that are there for your pleasure. Tune in to the sunrise, the little children, the laughter, the rain, and the birds. Drink it all in . . . there is no way to happiness; happiness is the way.

Dr. Wayne W. Dyer

1940–2015

EACH DAY has a rarity . . . I could put it in a vase and
admire it, like the first dandelions . . .

MARGARET LAURENCE
1926–1987

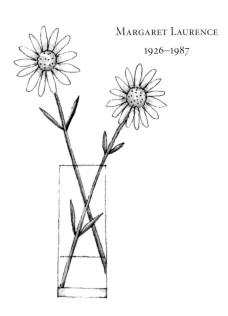

Exercise: Exploring Emotions

BE CURIOUS with mindfulness. As you breathe, notice any emotions or feelings you are experiencing. Notice, if you can, where these feelings are located—are they mostly in your head, throat, chest, or do you feel them in your gut and abdomen? If any thoughts come to you, be aware of them with curiosity, not judgment. Do this for a few minutes and then bring your awareness back to your breathing before you finish.

ENJOY THE blessings of the day . . . and the evils bear
patiently; for this day only is ours: we are dead to
yesterday, and not born to tomorrow.

JEREMY TAYLOR
1613–1667

I WISH that life should not be cheap, but sacred. I wish the days to be as centuries, loaded, fragrant.

RALPH WALDO EMERSON
1803–1882

THE MIND is flickering and restless,
difficult to guard, difficult to control.
The wise straightens the mind as a
fletcher straightens an arrow.

FROM *THE DHAMMAPADA*

YOU CAN'T earn, save or own happiness.
You can't buy it, trade it or sell it. It is an attitude.
An attitude of living. An appreciation of life,
of love. It can come to you. Just be yourself, be
mindful. Just be. Accept grace, accept love, accept
life. It'll come to you. Try it. You'll see.

DR. DALTON EXLEY

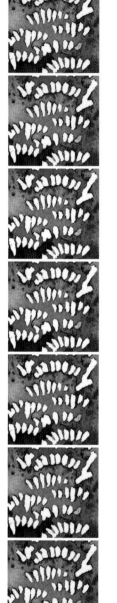

INFINITE WORLDS appear
and disappear in the wide
expanse of my consciousness,
like motes of dust dancing in
a heaven of light.

SANSKRIT SAYING

WHEN IS it right to be happy?
Right here—right now!

STUART & LINDA MACFARLANE

OUR LIFE is frittered
away with detail. . . .
Simplify, simplify.

HENRY DAVID THOREAU
1817–1862

KEEP COOL: it will be all one
a hundred years hence.

RALPH WALDO EMERSON
1803–1882

In this very breath
that we take now lies
the secret that all great
teachers try to tell us.

Peter Matthiessen
1927–2014

Outside noisy, inside empty.

Chinese saying

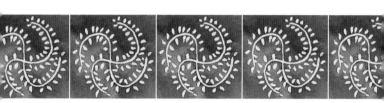

WHAT YOU have understood as true and good, just do that at once. What's the good of calculating what may or may not befall in future? The span of life is so, so short—and can anything be accomplished in it if you go on forecasting and computing results.

SWAMI VIVEKANANDA
1863–1902

YOU WERE made for enjoyment, and the world was
filled with things which you will enjoy . . .

JOHN RUSKIN
1819–1900

PEACE IS always beautiful.

WALT WHITMAN
1819–1892

WHEN YOU drink just drink,

when you walk just walk.

ZEN SAYING

IF YOU consider all the people you know who seem truly happy, there is likely to be one trait—one essential perspective on life—that each of these happy people share . . . It is the word now. It is the understanding that happiness exists at just one time. And that time is now.

WILLIE NELSON, B. 1933

MIND AND body are not separate entities. What affects one, affects the other. If you are too often anxious, worried and stressed, your body will suffer stress-related disorders. Become mindful, you will be healthier as well as happier for it.

DR. DALTON EXLEY

Remember to Practice Mindfulness Exercises

SIMPLY SIT comfortably and well-supported
in a chair. Close your eyes and become aware
of where your body is—your feet on the floor,
the backs of your legs against the chair, your
thighs, buttocks, and back. Notice any
sounds or smells. Breathe in and out.

SURELY THERE is something in the unruffled calm of
nature that overawes our little anxieties and doubts:
the sight of the deep blue sky, and the clustering stars
above, seem to impart a quiet to the mind.

JONATHAN EDWARDS
1703–1758

MAY WE all grow in grace and
peace, and not neglect the silence
that is in the center of our being.
It will not fail us.

THOMAS MERTON
1915–1968

THIS IS a way of liberation, concerned
not with discovering what is good or bad
or advantageous, but what is.

ALAN WATTS
1915–1973

DON'T PUT off today with talk of tomorrow.
Tomorrow you'll do this, you'll do that, you
will start your big plans tomorrow. No, live
now. Start this minute.

DR. DALTON EXLEY

Sometimes, as I drift idly on Walden Pond,
I cease to live and begin to be.

Henry David Thoreau
1817–1862

THE SENSE of existence is the greatest happiness.

BENJAMIN DISRAELI
1804–1881

. . . THERE IS joy for me, as ever, in not
moving at all, but just basking in the sun
at the allotment, watching the butterflies
start their summer dance, between the
buddleia and the ornamental grasses; and
reclining on my blue, stripy deckchair in
the front garden . . .

BARNEY BARDSLEY

Go—NOT knowing where.
Bring—not knowing what. The
path is long, the way unknown.

RUSSIAN FAIRY TALE

Don't fight with time—
it'll win. It will win. Don't
wish you were younger, or
older or somewhere else—live
now, love now.

Dr. Dalton Exley

Do NOT say, "It is morning,"
and dismiss it with a name of
yesterday. See it for the first
time as a newborn child that
has no name.

RABINDRANATH TAGORE
1861–1941

THERE WAS a blackbird in the garden, and it was as though there had never been a blackbird before. All my inner turmoil melted away and I felt full of clarity and inner peace. I seemed at one with everything around me …

ANNE BANCROFT
1931–2005

THE MORNING sun, the new sweet earth
and the great silence.

T. C. McLuhan

THE WHOLE life of man
is but a point of time;
let us enjoy it, therefore,
while it lasts.

PLUTARCH
A.D. 46–120

OUR COLLECTIVE fears and anxieties about
ourselves, our pasts, our futures, keep us from
enjoying now, enjoying being, enjoying the
simple pleasures of the day.

DR. DALTON EXLEY

IN THE midst of movement and chaos, keep stillness inside of you.

DEEPAK CHOPRA, B. 1946

AFTER A lovely day out of doors
by myself I saw that a single act of
admiration is of little use. We must live
with beauty, without any straining effort
to admire, quietly attentive, absorbent,
until by degrees the beauty becomes one
with us and alters our blood.

MARK RUTHERFORD
1831–1913

CATCH THE vigorous horse of your mind.

ZEN SAYING

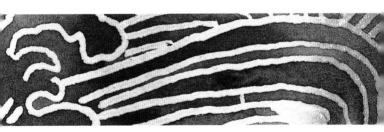

Now is the only time there is.
The present is all we have.

Eknath Easwaran
1910–1999

To BE interested in the changing seasons is a happier state of mind than to be hopelessly in love with spring.

GEORGE SANTAYANA

1863–1952

REST IS not idleness, and to lie sometimes on the grass under the trees on a Summer's day, listening to the murmur of water, or watching the clouds float across the sky, is by no means a waste of time.

SIR JOHN LUBBOCK
1834–1913

IF YOU concentrate on finding whatever is good
in every situation, you will discover that your life
will suddenly be filled with gratitude, a feeling that
nurtures the soul.

RABBI HAROLD KUSHNER, B. 1935

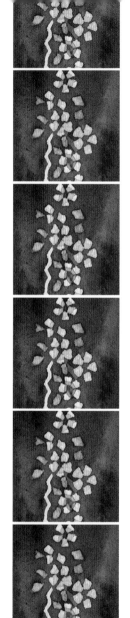

TAKE TIME TO dream—
It is hitching your wagon to a star.
Take time to love and to be loved—
Take time to look around—
It is too short a day to be closed in.
Take time to laugh—
It is the music of the soul.

FROM AN OLD ENGLISH SAMPLER

Exercise: Just Being in the Now

SIT OR lie down and direct your attention to the present moment. Calm your mind, remind yourself that all things pass. Sense your body, ask yourself if there is anywhere you can let go of tension, and release it. Let thoughts come into your mind, but just note them and any associated feelings—positive or negative—just observe them, observe yourself. Be aware of your body, your breath, your mind, your emotions. Accept this moment in time.

Close to the Earth

COME TO a quiet place,
A place so quiet
That you can hear
The grass grow.
Lie on the soft grass,
Run your fingers
Through the softness
Of its petals,
And listen:
Listen to the earth.
The warm earth,
The life pulse
Of us all.

ALICE TAYLOR, B. 1938

ADOPT THE pace of nature:

her secret is patience.

RALPH WALDO EMERSON

1803–1882

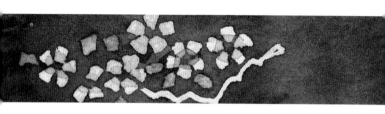

... THIS WAS the simple happiness of complete harmony with her surroundings, the happiness that asks for nothing, that just accepts, just breathes, just is.

COUNTESS ELIZABETH VON ARNIM
1866–1941

THINGS ARE entirely what they appear to be—
and behind them . . . there is nothing.

JEAN-PAUL SARTRE
1905–1980

NOBODY SEES a flower
really; it is so small. We
haven't time, and to see
takes time.

GEORGIA O'KEEFFE
1887–1986

ALL PRESENT beauty is
the only beauty.

HELEN EXLEY

Do NOT be antagonistic to the world of the senses. For when you are not antagonistic to it, it turns out to be the same as complete awakening.

Seng-Ts'an
529–606

SPEND ALL you have for loveliness,
Buy it and never count the cost;
For one white singing hour of peace
Count many a year of strife well lost,
And for a breath of ecstasy
Give all you have been, or could be.

SARA TEASDALE
1884–1933

EVEN THOUGH one masters various profound
teachings, it is like placing a single hair in vast space.
Even if one gains all the essential knowledge in the
world, it is like throwing a drop of water into
a deep ravine.

TE-SHAN
782–865

FEELINGS LIKE disappointment, embarrassment, irritation, resentment, anger, jealousy, and fear, instead of being bad news, are actually very clear moments that teach us where it is that we're holding back.

PEMA CHÖDRÖN, B. 1936

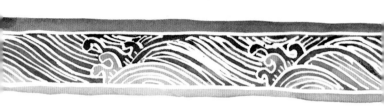

NEVER LET the future disturb you. You will meet it,
if you have to, with the same weapons of reason which
today arm you against the present.

MARCUS AURELIUS
121–180

I LOVE to spend time in nature, the wilder the better.
Still water, grass blown gently by the wind, silence.
Here with this precious time, the sun and the stars, the
wild enters. The wild . . . that isn't taxed with grief or
stress. Just this bright day. For a brief while I am free in
the grace of this world.

DR. DALTON EXLEY

WITHOUT STIRRING abroad one can
  know the whole world;
Without looking out of the window one
  can see the way of heaven.
The further one goes the less one knows.

LAO TZU
C. 604–531 B.C.

THIS DAY is for all that is good and fair. It is too dear, with its hopes and invitations, to waste a moment on yesterdays.

RALPH WALDO EMERSON
1803–1882

THERE IS beauty around us, in things large and small,
in friends, family, the countryside, a singing bird. Stop
to reflect, to give thanks, to contemplate the gift of
another day. Touch the wonders of life and rejoice.

ANTON CHEKHOV
1860–1904

A daily thought on being present in the now

TRUE HAPPINESS is . . . to enjoy the present, without
anxious dependence upon the future.

SENECA THE YOUNGER
4 B.C.–A.D. 65

JUST SLOW down. Slow down your speech. Slow down your breathing. Slow down your walking. Slow down your eating. And let this slower, steadier pace perfume your mind. Just slow down . . .

DOKO

LET GO of what you can't control.
Channel all that energy into living
fully in the NOW.

KAREN SALMANSOHN

PEOPLE SAY time flies. But if you are truly mindful time doesn't fly. It is constantly renewed, ever present with you, and there is the wonderful feeling that there is an eternity of time. Time for everything.

DR. DALTON EXLEY

OF COURSE mind and body are not
separate. So to be well, cultivate a
healthy body and a healthy mind.

DR. DALTON EXLEY

ONE MUST never look for happiness:

one meets it by the way . . .

ISABELLE EBERHARDT

1877–1904

Joy is the realization of
the truth of oneness, the
oneness of our soul with
the world and of the
world-soul . . .

Rabindranath Tagore
1861–1941

HAPPINESS, NOT in another place but this place . . .
not for another hour, but this hour.

WALT WHITMAN
1819–1892

"IF IT were just a matter
of playing football with the
firmament, stirring up the
ocean, turning back rivers,
carrying away mountains,
I could manage it easily
enough," said Monkey. "But
if it comes to sitting still and
meditating, I am bound to
come off badly. It's quite
against my nature to sit still."

WU CHENG'EN
1500–1582

The Basic Mindful Exercise

THE BASIC mindful exercise is to breathe in and breathe out. Do it often. And sometimes do it an extra time—perhaps where and when you've never done it before. If any thoughts arise, notice them, but don't be judgmental or try and change anything, or "do" anything. Just notice, just be aware. Notice any tensions, tightness or other sensations in your body. Sense the world around you.

MIND IS the forerunner of all good states. Our life is the creation of our mind. If one speaks or acts with pure mind, happiness follows one as his own shadow that never leaves.

FROM *THE DHAMMAPADA*

WHY IS it that I find it so
hard to take time for myself? Time to
be, rather than time to do. And often what
is urgent elbows its way to the forefront
of my day and the important gets
trampled in the rush.

MARION STROUD
1940–2015

EVERY NOW and again take a good look at
something not made with hands—a mountain, a star,
the turn of a stream. There will come to you
wisdom and patience and solace.

SIDNEY LOVETT
1890–1979

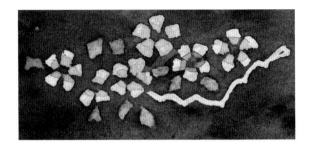

MINDFULNESS IS being aware of yourself,
others, and your surroundings in the moment.
When consciously and kindly focusing awareness
on life as it unfolds minute by precious minute,
you are better able to savor each experience.

SUE PATTON THOELE, B. 1940

A daily thought on being present in the now

EACH DAY provides its own gifts.

MARTIAL

C. A.D. 40–C. 104

EVERYTHING IN the end passes.
Everything in your life in the end
passes. Celebrate your existence
while you have it! Every day. All that
you love, all that you live for, these
are the things that matter. Yes, be
mindful. Yes, of course be mindful
and live your life to the full.

DR. DALTON EXLEY

THIS IS the real secret of life—to be completely engaged with what you are doing in the here and now. And instead of calling it work, realize it is play.

ALAN WATTS

1915–1973

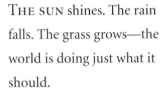

THE SUN shines. The rain falls. The grass grows—the world is doing just what it should.

STUART & LINDA MACFARLANE

TRUE JOY is serene.

SENECA THE YOUNGER
4 B.C.–A.D. 65

To WHAT shall
I compare this
life of ours? Even
before I can say it
is like a lightning
flash or a dewdrop
it is no more.

SENGAI
1750–1837

LIVING IN the present. With the past, I have nothing to do; nor with the future. I live now.

RALPH WALDO EMERSON
1803–1882

You MUST live in the present, launch yourself on every wave, find your eternity in each moment. Fools stand on their island of opportunities and look toward another land. There is no other land; there is no other life but this.

HENRY DAVID THOREAU
1817–1862

LOOK AT the sky. Look at the river.
Look at the trees. Feel, Touch, Smell. It
all belongs to you. You are part of this
wonderful creation.

STUART & LINDA MACFARLANE

A Standing Mindfulness Exercise

STAND STILL for a while, noticing how your body connects to the ground. Become aware of your surroundings, the sights, sounds and smells. Notice, but don't try to change your breath as it moves in and out. You can do this when you want during the day.

IT IS so, so liberating when we let go of the feeling of being ruled, being tied to time. Releasing the stress we get about what time it is, about what we have to do in what space of time. It is our choice ultimately, to be stressed by time or not to be.

DR. DALTON EXLEY

THE HIGHEST point a person
can attain is not Knowledge, or
Virtue, or Goodness, or Victory,
but something even greater, more
heroic, and more despairing:
Sacred Awe!

NIKOS KAZANTZAKIS
1883–1957

PARADISE IS where I am.

VOLTAIRE

1694–1778

ONE CANNOT appreciate beauty on the run. When I can be motionless long enough, there is no limit I have ever reached to the revelations in an opening bud.

VIDA D. SCUDDER
1861–1954

Among the mind's powers is one that comes of itself to many children and artists. It need not be lost, to the end of our days, by anyone who has ever had it. This is the power of taking delight in a thing, or rather in anything, not as a means to some other end, but just because it is what it is. A child in the full health of his mind will put his hand flat on the summer turf, feel it, and give a little shiver of private glee at the elastic firmness of the globe.

Charles Edward Montague
1867–1928

IT'S FUNNY how hard people find it to just be. We are so conditioned that we must be "getting on with things," to be always working, doing something, striving, stressing about money, about being more successful, about attaining "the next step."

DR. DALTON EXLEY

A daily thought on being present in the now

TIME IS but the stream I go a-fishing in.

HENRY DAVID THOREAU

1817–1862

FOREVER IS composed
of nows.

EMILY DICKINSON
1830–1886

FORGET ABOUT enlightenment. Sit down wherever you are and listen to the wind that is singing in your veins.

JOHN WELWOOD, B. 1943

Don't mortgage today
for the promise of a better life
tomorrow. Plan for the future?
Yes, yes, of course, but live
today, live each day.

D. E. Harold

. . . I KEEP trying gently to
bring my mind back to what
is really there to be seen,
maybe to be seen and noted
with a kind of reverence.

ANNE LAMOTT, B. 1954

TRUE BEAUTY must come, must
be grown, from within.

RALPH W. TRINE
1866–1958

SILENCE, PEACE and calm—so rare in this hectic world we live in. Find your moments, a brief and precious respite from the unrelenting, roaring pace of human endeavor. Cherish these moments. Take them when you can.

DR. DALTON EXLEY

THERE CAN be no very black misery to those who live
in the midst of nature and have their senses still.

HENRY DAVID THOREAU
1817–1862

Exercise: Listening Mindfully

THIS EXERCISE helps you broaden your appreciation of sound. It works best if you choose a piece of music you don't know; you could listen to the radio or put on headphones. Close your eyes and really listen to the music. Try not to judge it by genre or artist, ignore these labels and just listen to the sound. Pick out different instruments; give yourself permission to let go of preconceptions and get lost in the sound.

WHAT COULD be more therapeutic than to work outside in the fresh air, feeling wind, sun or rain beating on your skin, and driving the real, lovely world into your heart?

BARNEY BARDSLEY

A HAPPY life is not built up of tours
abroad and pleasant holidays, but of
little clumps of violets noticed
by the roadside.

DR. EDWARD A. WILSON
1872–1912

At a certain point you say to the woods, to the sea, to the mountains, to the world, Now I am ready. Now I will stop and be wholly attentive. You empty yourself and wait, listening. After a time you hear it: there is nothing there. There is nothing but those things only, those created objects, discrete, growing or holding, or swaying, or being rained on or raining, held, flooding or ebbing, standing, or spread. You feel the world's word as a tension, a hum, a single chorused note everywhere the same. This is it: this hum is the silence.

Annie Dillard, b. 1945

I AM calmest when I am at my ranch. This is where I
am able to forget about the pressures of being Pelé, and
I can for a time just be Edson. I rest. I relax. Thoughts
about life, my obligations and the responsibilities
I've gained, disappear. I like looking after the fish, the
horses and even the pigs. I'm in touch with nature, and
I enjoy the peace and quiet tremendously.

PELÉ, B. 1940

You never enjoy the world aright till the sea itself floweth in your veins, till you are clothed with the heavens and crowned with the stars.

Thomas Traherne
1636–1674

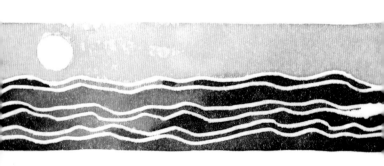

TODAY MORTGAGED for tomorrow. The years go by, lost forever in time, before one day we wake up and realize we only ever had today, that somehow we have lost our way a bit, lost the grace of life, the beauty of time, the happiness of a child.

DR. DALTON EXLEY

Mindfulness and Serious Difficulties

START BY being aware of your breathing. Then focus on what's distressing you. Take time to notice the tightening or tension in your body. See if you can put words to the painful thoughts that may be linked to anger, fear, loneliness or hurt. Don't try to change things, just be interested and aware—as if your best friend was explaining what was troubling them. To close, bring your attention back to your breathing.

MINDFULNESS IS being alive fully in the now. Not wishing to change it and clouding it with our anxieties, our phobias, our obsessions and our stresses.

HAROLD DALTON

THE ACKNOWLEDGMENT of impermanence holds
within it the key to life itself.

STEPHEN LEVINE
1937–2016

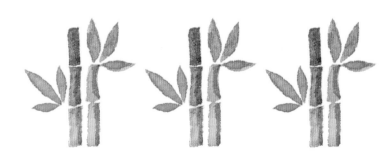

THE DREAM was always
running ahead of one.
To catch up, to live for a
moment in unison with it,
that was the miracle.

ANAÏS NIN
1903–1977

LIVE THIS actual moment,
only this. Yesterdays and
tomorrows exist largely in
your head. Live each moment
fully and the tomorrows will
look after themselves.

DR. DALTON EXLEY

SUDDENLY THE heart lifts with joy—finding itself part of all that is. Sunlight and cloud, trees, rivers, wild geese flying. A moment's glory.

CHARLOTTE GRAY
1937–2014

SIMPLY BE. Be aware of what is happening right now.
Stop dreaming about how your life might be different.
Don't continually deny the present. Enjoy the now.
Enjoy each day. Enjoy the journey.

D. E. HAROLD

Have much and be confused.

Lao Tzu

c. 604–531 b.c.

BE GLAD today, tomorrow may bring tears;

Be brave today, the darkest night will pass,

And golden rays will usher in the dawn;

Who conquers now shall rule the coming years.

SARAH KNOWLES BOLTON

1841–1916

BEAUTY IS all around us every day. In a million ways. When we release ourselves from endlessly planning and worrying, it is as if we can see again for the first time.

DR. DALTON EXLEY

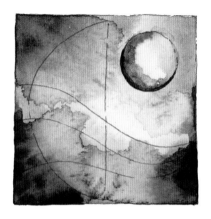

LIVE IN each season as it passes, breathe the air, drink the drink, taste the fruit, and resign yourself to the influences of each.

HENRY DAVID THOREAU
1817–1862

LEARN TO be silent. Let your mind listen and absorb.

PYTHAGORAS

C. 570–C. 500 B.C.

LET US not look back in anger, nor forward in fear, but around us in awareness.

JAMES THURBER
1894–1961

HE DID each single thing
as if he did nothing else.

CHARLES DICKENS
1812–1870

We look backward too much and we look forward too much; thus we miss the only eternity of which we can be absolutely sure—the eternal present, for it is always now.

William Lyon Phelps
1865–1943

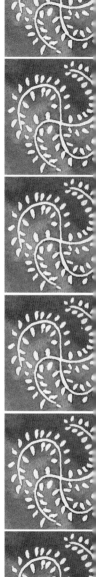

LIFE IS but momentary, whether you have the poverty of the poorest person in rags or the wealth of the richest living person. Life is but momentary, whether you have the best of health or the worst. Life is but momentary, whether you have the most poetical temperament or the most cruel.

SWAMI VIVEKANANDA
1863–1902

IT IS eternity now. I am in the midst of it. It is about me in the sunshine; I am in it, as the butterfly floats in the light-laden air. Nothing has to come; it is now. Now is eternity.

RICHARD JEFFERIES
1848–1887

. . . BEING CLOSELY attentive gives you the opportunity to change unwise or painful feelings and responses quickly. In fact, being truly present in a mindful way is an excellent stress reducer and, because of that, can be seen as consciousness conditioning, a strengthening workout for body, mind, heart, and spirit.

SUE PATTON THOELE,
B. 1940

Nothing is worth more
than this day.

Johann Wolfgang von Goethe
1749–1832

THE MIND is never right
but when it is at peace
within itself.

SENECA THE YOUNGER
4 B.C.–A.D. 65

ENJOY THE brief beautiful flash of life as it passes by
and through you, the light, the flowers, the love you
give and the love you receive.

DR. DALTON EXLEY

STOP ACTING as if life is a rehearsal.
Live this day as if it were your last.
The past is over and gone. The future
is not guaranteed.

DR. WAYNE W. DYER
1940–2015

WE ARE here and it is now. Further than that all
human knowledge is moonshine.

H. L. MENCKEN
1880–1956

THE AIR is full of sounds, sighs of the wind in the trees, sighs which fade back into the overhanging silence. A bee passes, a golden ripple in the quiet air.

MARION MILNER
1900–1998

. . . WHILE OTHERS miserably pledge themselves to
the insatiable pursuit of ambition and brief power,
I will be stretched out in the shade, singing.

FRAY LUIS DE LEÓN
1527–1591

To WHAT shall I liken the world?
Moonlight, reflected in dewdrops,
Shaken from a crane's bill.

ZEN MASTER DOGEN
1200–1253

We push our children ever harder, urging them to sacrifice their todays for imagined tomorrows. Yet, when asked, we wish for them most happiness in their lives.

Dr. Dalton Exley

WHEN ANXIETY hovers above your light and shadows
and all your actions, please do not fear them too much.
I would like to remind you that life has not forgotten
you. It is holding you by your hand and will not let
you fall. Why do you want to shut out of your life any
uneasiness or any depression? For after all, even though
you do not know now where all of this will lead, these
experiences may lead to the change that you were
always hoping for.

RAINER MARIA RILKE
1875–1926

HAVE MORE than thou showest,
Speak less than thou knowest.

WILLIAM SHAKESPEARE
1564–1616

THINK OF what does not think. How do you think of what does not think? It is not thinking. This is the essential art of sitting Zen meditation.

ZEN MASTER DOGEN
1200–1253

Do NOT dwell in
the past, do not
dream of the future,
concentrate the
mind on the present
moment.

GAUTAMA BUDDHA
C. 563–483 B.C.

A Mindful Appreciation Exercise

PICK FIVE things you think usually go unappreciated in your daily life. They could be things like the electricity that powers your home, the trees in your local park, or the school that teaches your children. Or the air we all breathe. Have you ever stopped to think how these things benefit us all? How life would be without them?

YESTERDAY HAS gone. Tomorrow may never come.
There is only the miracle of this moment.
Savor it. It is a gift.

MARIE STILKIND

THE FALL of a leaf is a whisper to the living.

RUSSIAN PROVERB

No "What ifs,"
no "if onlys,"
just LIVE . . . today.

Jane Drury

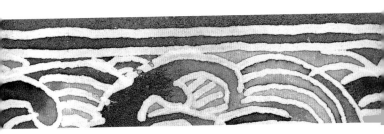

THE PERSON is richest who is
content with the least.

SOCRATES

469–399 B.C.

ENJOY LIFE, employ life.
It flits away and will not stay.

PROVERB

YOU ASK why I make my home in the
mountain forest, and I smile, and am silent,
and even my soul remains quiet: it lives in
the other world which no one owns. The
peach trees blossom. The water flows.

LI PO
701–762

WE KNOW nothing of tomorrow; our business is to be
good and happy today.

SYDNEY SMITH

1771–1845

THE ONE who has conquered himself is a far greater hero than he who has defeated a thousand times a thousand men.

FROM *THE DHAMMAPADA*

Don't seek, don't search, don't ask, don't knock,
don't demand—relax.

Osho

1931–1990

AN INCH of time is an inch of gold:
Treasure it.
Appreciate its fleeting nature;
Misplaced gold is easily found, misspent time
is lost forever.

LOY CHING-YUEN

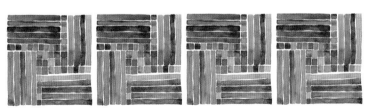

LOOK AT everything as though you
were seeing it either for the first or
last time. Then your time will be
filled with glory.

BETTY SMITH

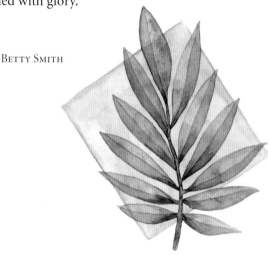

TO BE enlightened is to be one with
all things.

ZEN MASTER DOGEN

1200–1253

WHAT IS Life? It is the flash
of a firefly in the night.
It is the breath of a buffalo
in the winter time. It is the
little shadow which runs
across the grass and loses
itself in the sunset.

CROWFOOT,
BLACKFOOT INDIAN LEADER
1830–1890

THE REAL discovery is not finding new landscapes,
but in having new eyes.

MARCEL PROUST
1871–1922

For a little while put down your ambitions, unburden yourself of your dreams. Be in the moment. Enjoy it for what it is. The future can wait—this is the time for now!

Stuart & Linda Macfarlane

WHEN I dance, I dance; when I sleep,
I sleep; yes, and when I walk alone in a
beautiful orchard, if my thoughts drift to
far-off matters I lead them back again to
the walk, the orchard, to the sweetness of
this solitude, to myself.

MICHEL EYQUEM DE MONTAIGNE
1533–1592

FINISH EACH day and be done with it. You have done what you could; some blunders and absurdities no doubt crept in; forget them as soon as you can. Tomorrow is a new day; you shall begin it serenely, and with too high a spirit to be encumbered with your own nonsense.

RALPH WALDO EMERSON
1803–1882

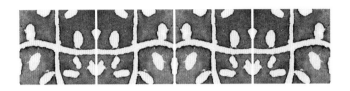

I AM grateful for what I am and have. My thanksgiving is perpetual. It is surprising how contented one can be with nothing definite—only a sense of existence. My breath is sweet to me. O, how I laugh when I think of my vague indefinite riches. No run on my bank can drain it, for my wealth is not possession but enjoyment.

HENRY DAVID THOREAU
1817–1862

OUR ORIGINAL nature is, in the
highest truth, void, silent, pure;
it is glorious and mysterious
peaceful joy—and that is all. Enter
deeply into it by awakening to it
yourself. That which is before you
is it, in all its fullness,
utterly complete.

HUANG PO, D. 850

LOST YESTERDAY, somewhere between sunrise and sunset, two golden hours, each set with sixty diamond minutes. No reward is offered, for they are gone forever.

LYDIA H. SIGOURNEY
1791–1865

THE SECRET of seeing things as they are is to take off our colored spectacles. That being-as-it-is, with nothing extraordinary about it, nothing wonderful, is the great wonder.

MASTER SESSAN

Mindful Awareness Exercise

THIS BEING-IN-THE-NOW exercise is designed to cultivate an appreciation of simple everyday tasks. Think of something you do regularly, like using a computer, or washing your clothes. Appreciate your brain as it facilitates your understanding and your hands that enable you to use the tools. Doing this awareness exercise on each of your usual tasks will stop you from functioning so much on autopilot.

THE QUIETER you
become the more
you can hear.

BABA RAM DASS, B. 1931

FEAR NOT for the future;

weep not for the past.

PERCY BYSSHE SHELLEY

1792–1822

THE FUTURE is always beginning

now.

MARK STRAND

1934–2014

LOOK TO this day! Look to this day!
For it is life, the very life of life. In its
brief course lie all the varieties and
realities of your existence: the bliss
of growth, the glory of action, the
splendor of beauty. For yesterday is
already a dream and tomorrow is only
a vision, but today, well-lived, makes
every yesterday a dream of happiness,
and every tomorrow a vision of hope.
Look well, therefore, to this day!
Such is the salutation of the dawn.

SANSKRIT SAYING

CARPENTERS BEND wood;
fletchers bend arrows;
wise people fashion themselves.

GAUTAMA BUDDHA
C. 563–483 B.C.

MY ADVICE to you is not to inquire why or whither,
but just enjoy your ice cream while it's on your plate—
that's my philosophy.

THORNTON WILDER
1897–1975

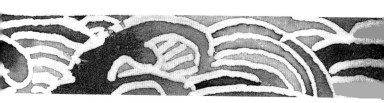

Happiness may only last
a fraction of an hour. But it
stays inside the heart beyond
all time.

E. Wright

GOOD HEAVENS, of what uncostly material is our earthly happiness composed . . . if we only knew it. What incomes have we not had from a flower, and how unfailing are the dividends of the seasons.

JAMES RUSSELL LOWELL
1819–1891

IT IS POSSIBLE to lose money, wealth, position, status, friends, even love and win these back. Time is the one thing you can never win back. Spend each minute wisely. Enjoy your time. You will never get it back again.

DR. DALTON EXLEY

Silence desire, ambition and anxiety.
Be still.

Pam Brown
1928–2014

REALITY IS a flowing. This does not mean that everything moves, changes, becomes. Science and common experience tell us that. It means that movement, change, becoming is everything that there is. There is nothing else; everything is movement, is change. The time that we ordinarily think about is not real time, but a picture of space.

HENRY-LOUIS BERGSON

1859–1941

FOR AFTER all, the best
thing one can do when it is
raining is to let it rain.

HENRY WADSWORTH LONGFELLOW
1807–1882

SIMPLE PLEASURES . . . are the last refuge
of the complex.

OSCAR WILDE
1854–1900

IN THIS moment, there is
plenty of time. In this moment,
you are precisely as you should
be. In this moment, there is
infinite possibility.

VICTORIA MORAN,
B. 1950

THERE IS no need to run outside for better seeing.
Nor to peer from a window. Rather abide at the
center of your being; for the more you leave it
the less you learn.

LAO TZU

C. 604–531 B.C.

IT NEVER ends. It becomes an endless process: you and nature have become one and you borrow its infinitude. You then have to go back again and again, because each time you outgrow, in some way, the self you were before.

JANE HOLLISTER WHEELWRIGHT

1905–2004

To TRULY be calm you need to live in the moment without care for the next moment or regret for the previous moment.

STUART & LINDA MACFARLANE

WHATEVER THE present moment
contains, accept it as if you had chosen it.
Always work with it, not against it.

ECKHART TOLLE, B. 1948

THERE IS no beyond, there is only here, the infinitely small, infinitely great and utterly demanding present.

IRIS MURDOCH
1919–1999

Mindfulness Walking Exercise

FIND A quiet space where you can walk a bit and remove your shoes. Begin slowly walking, only taking twelve steps. Be attentive to how you transfer weight, how you move over the ground, the sensations in your feet, your legs, your back, your torso, your arms, your neck, your head. Walk with awareness, stop and turn around and walk back. Practice this walking mindfulness.

SPEAK NOUGHT, move not, but listen,
   the sky is full of gold.
No ripple on the river, no stir in field or fold,
All gleams but nought doth glisten,
   but the far off unseen sea.

Forget days past, heart broken, put all
   memory by!
No grief on the green hillside, no pity
   in the sky,
Joy that may not be spoken fills
   mead and flower and tree.

WILLIAM MORRIS
1834–1896

START LIVING in the present moment. Stop dwelling on the past or worrying about the future. That's mindfulness and it is so freeing.

DR. DALTON EXLEY

IF MY heart can become pure and simple like
that of a child, I think there probably can be
no greater happiness than this.

KITARO NISHIDA
1870–1945

WE ARE in danger of drowning—in trivia, in chattering, in a swirl, a mounting tide, a great tsunami of gabble. Find higher ground. Find happiness. Find peace.

PAM BROWN

1928–2014

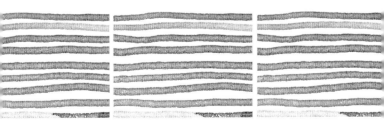

THERE EXISTS only the present instant . . . a Now which always and without end is itself new. There is no yesterday nor any tomorrow, but only Now, as it was a thousand years ago and as it will be a thousand years since.

MEISTER ECKHART
C. 1260–C. 1327

I LIVE in the present, and it is such a luxurious feeling, a hot bath of the soul. Life is a place where there is no time to lose, no reason to be bored.

BRIGITTE MUIR, B. 1958

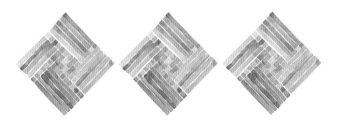

Try looking at your mind as a wayward puppy that you are trying to paper train. You don't drop-kick a puppy into the neighbor's yard every time it piddles on the floor. You just keep bringing it back to the newspaper.

ANNE LAMOTT, B. 1954

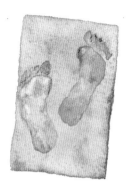

MAKE YOUR peace with life, with this world and everything in it. Truly do this. If you actually do this you will hardly need to even think about practicing mindfulness, it will be like your heart beating or your breathing—completely natural. Like a function of living, nothing to be done . . .

DR. DALTON EXLEY

THE WAY to use life is to do nothing through acting.
The way to use life is to do everything through being.

LAO TZU
C. 604–531 B.C.

The Mindful Immersion Exercise

THIS EXERCISE is about escaping from the constant stress and strivings of our daily routines and cultivating an appreciation, a contentment in being. It's a challenge to choose a regular chore you don't particularly like: clearing up or doing the vacuuming. Instead of rushing the job, try relaxing into it, taking your time and immersing yourself in it. You might surprise yourself by actually enjoying clearing up; you never know!

TIME AND again we miss out on
the great treasures in our lives
because we are so restless.
In our minds we are always
elsewhere. We are seldom in
the place where we stand and
in the time that is now.

JOHN O'DONOHUE
1956–2008

I DON'T know if you can live inside each and every moment. But when you can, try to stop, look, and listen long enough to be right where you are, not in your past, not in your future. Just right in the middle of a split second in time.

LESLIE LEVINE

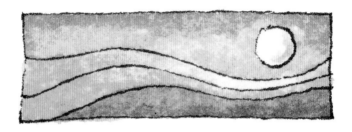

IF YOU want to be happy, be.

LEO TOLSTOY
1828–1910

WHEN I live in the now, I feel no real pain from the past. Imagined fear of the future can't harm me.

JOAN BURKA

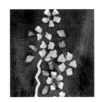 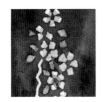 

NONE OF us is promised tomorrow.
Today, in all its beauty and sadness and
complexity, is all we have. This light we
see may be the last such day we have on
this earth. There is no certainty, beyond
the fact that one day we will have no
tomorrow, and that it is not ours to
know when that day will be.

KENT NERBURN, B. 1946

SOMETIMES I listen to the silence,
gaze at the light falling on a plaster
wall, a patch of woody grass or the
clouds moving across a tumbled sky . . .
At such moments I am released from
dependence on the future and to have
no longings to be other than where I am.

JOHN LANE
1930–2012

LIE GENTLY in the dark and listen to the rain pattering against the glass, the swish of passing cars, the hush of leaves. Renounce decisions, speculation, the tug of time. The world beyond the window enfolds your silence, holds you softly. Sleep.

PAM BROWN

1928–2014

WE CAN easily manage, if we only take each day, the burden appointed for it. But the load will be too heavy for us if we carry yesterday's burden over again today, and then add the burden of the morrow to the weight before we are required to bear it.

JOHN NEWTON
1725–1807

I DO not fear tomorrow, for
I have seen yesterday—
and I love today.

WILLIAM ALLEN WHITE
1868–1944

THEY HAD all lain still, thinking about this for a while. Somewhere, a long way off, a coyote called. "I guess that's all forever is," his father replied. "Just one long trail of nows. And I guess all you can do is try and live one now at a time without getting too worked up about the last now or the next now."

NICHOLAS EVANS, B. 1950

WE ALL experience "soul moments" in life—when we see a magnificent sunrise, hear the call of a loon, see the wrinkles in our mother's hand, or smell the sweetness of a baby. During these moments, our body, as well as our brain, resonates as we experience the glory of being a human being.

MARION WOODMAN
1928–2018

PERHAPS THIS very instant is your
time . . . your own, your peculiar,
your promised and presaged moment,
out of all moments forever.

LOUISE BOGAN
1897–1970

ONLY WHEN you have no thing in
your mind and no mind in things are
you vacant and spiritual, empty
and marvelous.

TOKUSAN, D. 865

ALL YOU really need to do is accept this
moment fully. You are then at ease in the
here and now at least with yourself.

ECKHART TOLLE, B. 1948

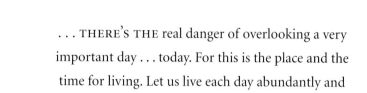

. . . THERE'S THE real danger of overlooking a very important day . . . today. For this is the place and the time for living. Let us live each day abundantly and beautifully while it is here.

ESTHER BALDWIN YORK

WE HAVE only now, only this single eternal moment opening and unfolding before us, day and night.

JACK KORNFIELD, B. 1945

THE ULTIMATE value of life
depends upon awareness and the
power of contemplation rather than
upon mere survival.

ARISTOTLE
384–322 B.C.

COME BACK to square one, just the minimum bare bones. Relaxing with the present moment, relaxing with hopelessness, relaxing with death, not resisting the fact that things end, that things pass, that things have no lasting substance, that everything is changing all the time.

PEMA CHÖDRÖN, B. 1936

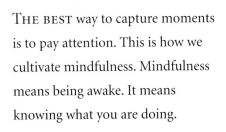

THE BEST way to capture moments is to pay attention. This is how we cultivate mindfulness. Mindfulness means being awake. It means knowing what you are doing.

JON KABAT-ZINN, B. 1944

BE AWARE of impermanence, because life is short and everything we do counts. Family relationships and friendships are precious beyond measure. If only we could live our life as if each moment were our last— opening and accepting the as-it-is-ness, the nature of reality.

CHAGDUD TULKU RINPOCHE
1930–2002

I am beginning to learn that it is the sweet, simple
things of life which are the real ones after all.

Laura Ingalls Wilder
1867–1957

IF THERE is to be any peace it will come through being, not having.

HENRY MILLER

1891–1980

THERE ARE only two ways to live your life. One is as though nothing is a miracle. The other is as though everything is a miracle.

ALBERT EINSTEIN
1879–1955

LET YOURSELF be silently drawn by the strange pull of
what you really love. It will not lead you astray.

JALAL AD-DIN MUHAMMAD RUMI

1207–1273

IN ORDER to swim one takes off all one's clothes—in order to aspire to the truth one must undress in a far more inward sense, divest oneself of all one's inward clothes, of thoughts, conceptions, selfishness, etc., before one is sufficiently naked.

SØREN KIERKEGAARD
1813–1855

IN THE depth of winter, I finally learned that within
me there lay an invincible summer.

ALBERT CAMUS
1913–1960

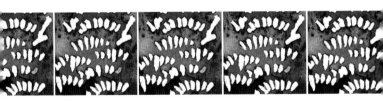

SIMPLIFYING OUR lives does not
mean sinking into idleness, but on
the contrary, getting rid of the most
subtle aspect of laziness: the one
which makes us take on thousands
of less important activities.

MATTHIEU RICARD, B. 1946

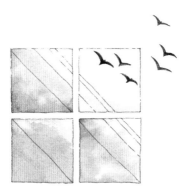

WRITE IT on your heart that every day
is the best day of the year.

RALPH WALDO EMERSON
1803–1882